# 101 TRIVIA QUESTIONS
# ABOUT LIONEL MESSI

A BIOGRAPHY OF ESSENTIAL FACTS AND STORIES
YOU NEED TO KNOW!

FAME FOCUS

# CONTENTS

# INTRODUCTION

Welcome to *101 Trivia Questions About Lionel Messi!* This book is a treasure trove of fascinating insights, stories, and trivia about one of the most iconic figures in the world of soccer, Lionel Messi. As a player who has mesmerized fans with his skills, determination, and remarkable achievements on the soccer pitch, Messi's journey from the humble streets of Rosario to global stardom is nothing short of inspirational.

Embark on a journey through the life of a soccer legend, exploring his early days, illustrious career, personal life, and the impact he has made both on and off the field. Each trivia question in this book is carefully crafted to test your knowledge and deepen your understanding of this extraordinary athlete.

Messi, a living legend in the world of soccer, is still actively writing his extraordinary story. While this book was finished in October 2023, he continues to captivate audiences and set new standards in the sport. It's important to note that the facts and statistics within this book are accurate as of this date. With his career ongoing, Messi's journey is an evolving saga, promising the possibility of more records to be shattered and more exhilarating chapters yet to unfold.

Get ready to dive into the world of Lionel Messi, a journey through the life of a man who has become more than just a soccer player, but a symbol of dedication, excellence, and unparalleled success.

# 1

## INSIDE THE WORLD OF SOCCER

Before delving into Lionel Messi's extraordinary soccer journey, it's crucial to gain insights into the broader soccer landscape that has served as the backdrop to his illustrious career. In this section, we will explore the pivotal facets of the soccer world that have shaped his narrative. We'll delve into the significance of the Ballon d'Or, the thrill of La Liga, the prestige of the UEFA European Championship, the fervor of El Clásico, the global allure of the FIFA World Cup, and the rich heritage of the Copa América. Understanding the importance of these competitions and accolades is essential to truly appreciate Messi's journey and achievements. They transcend mere tournaments or awards; they symbolize the pinnacle of a sport cherished by millions worldwide. As we delve into Messi's story in the subsequent pages, this foundation will enable us to fully grasp the extent of his impact on soccer and its storied history.

## Ballon d'Or

The Ballon d'Or stands as one of the most esteemed individual honors within the realm of soccer. It is an annual accolade bestowed by France Football magazine upon the  world's premier male soccerer, determined through the votes of a distinguished panel comprising international journalists, national team coaches, national team captains, and managers.

This award boasts a storied history, tracing its origins back to 1956 when it was inaugurated. Originally, the scope was limited to European players who were active in European clubs. However, in 1995, the eligibility criteria underwent an expansion, welcoming players from across the globe, irrespective of their playing location.

The Ballon d'Or serves as a testament to exceptional individual performances over the course of a calendar year, evaluating a player's contributions to both their club and national team. The selection process considers a range of attributes, including skill, consistency, leadership qualities, and the impact a player has had on the game. This distinction holds immense significance in the world of soccer, serving as an esteemed symbol of excellence and garnering immense desire from players, as it symbolizes recognition of their innate talent and remarkable accomplishments on the soccer field.

**El Clásico**

El Clásico transcends the status of a mere soccer match; it embodies a legendary rivalry between FC Barcelona and Real Madrid, constituting a historic and fiercely contested clash that has enraptured fans since the early 20th century. This enduring feud, renowned as one of the most highly anticipated showdowns in global soccer, extends far beyond the sport itself. The encounters between Barcelona and Real Madrid are monumental occasions, marked by immense stakes, fervent emotions, and unparalleled competition. These fixtures emerge as cultural phenomena that frequently cleave families, cities, and even nations along the lines of soccering allegiance.

The global magnetism of El Clásico is truly staggering, captivating fans worldwide. It serves not just as a display of extraordinary player prowess but also as a platform for showcasing the distinct soccering philosophies and traditions upheld by these two iconic clubs. Over the years, soccer legends such as Lionel Messi, Alfredo Di Stéfano, and Johan Cruyff have graced this rivalry, each contributing unforgettable performances that have further elevated the match's prestige.

Beyond the confines of the pitch, El Clásico bears substantial cultural significance in Spain, embodying the diverse identities of the nation. Barcelona and Real Madrid represent more than mere soccer entities; they symbolize regional pride and political intricacies, with Barcelona often tied to Catalonia and Real Madrid to the Spanish capital.

These fixtures are occasions where passion, skill, and drama seamlessly converge, captivating the hearts of both ardent soccer enthusiasts and casual viewers alike. Whether unfolding at Barcelona's Camp Nou or Madrid's Santiago Bernabéu, these stadiums morph into grand stages upon which some of soccer's most memorable narratives are woven, rendering El Clásico an authentic spectacle in the realm of sports.

## La Liga

 La Liga, also known as the Spanish Football League, boasts a storied history spanning nearly a century, with its origins tracing back to its establishment in 1929. It proudly stands as one of Europe's most ancient soccer leagues, steeped in tradition and holding immense significance within the Spanish soccer landscape.

Comprising 20 teams, La Liga embarks on an arduous season running from August to May, with each team engaging in 38 matches, featuring both home and away fixtures against every other team. La Liga is celebrated for its captivating and technically sophisticated style of play, home to iconic clubs such as FC Barcelona and Real Madrid, whose fierce rivalry in the legendary "El Clásico" commands global attention. The league's allure extends well beyond Spain's borders, captivating fans worldwide with its abundance of top-tier talent and high-caliber soccer.

On the European stage, La Liga clubs, including Barcelona, Real Madrid, and Atlético Madrid, have consistently demonstrated excellence, cementing their status as European soccer powerhouses in prestigious tournaments like the UEFA Champions League and UEFA Europa League. Within Spain itself, La Liga occupies a significant cultural position, with soccer deeply entrenched as a passion. League matches serve as a pivotal component of the nation's sporting and social calendar, underscoring the profound influence of soccer on Spanish society.

Furthermore, La Liga has played a vital role in the global expansion of soccer's popularity, elevating Spanish soccer to a prominent position and spreading the love for the game to diverse corners of the world.

## Copa América

The Copa América, established in 1916, stands as a venerable testament to the rich soccer history of South America, proudly holding the distinction of being the world's  oldest international soccer competition. This prestigious tournament has played an instrumental role in shaping the continent's soccer landscape, deeply steeped in tradition and impassioned fervor.

Held biennially, the Copa América convenes the foremost national teams from South América in a fiercely competitive and passionate display of soccer excellence. It garners acclaim for its capacity to showcase the continent's time-honored soccer traditions and exceptional talents, captivating fans not only across South America but also around the world with each edition. The tournament is renowned for igniting intense rivalries, with matches often brimming with heightened emotions. Legendary matchups such as Brazil vs. Argentina, famously known as the "Superclásico de las Américas," and Uruguay vs. Argentina in the "Clásico del Río de la Plata," resonate deeply with fans and add to the tournament's allure.

While primarily a South American affair, the Copa América has cast a global net, attracting an international audience drawn to its high level of play and the presence of world-class talent. It offers soccer enthusiasts worldwide a precious opportunity to witness some of the sport's most exceptional players in action.

**UEFA European Championship**

Since its inaugural edition in 1960, the UEFA European Championship, commonly known as the Euro, has occupied a central position in the realm of soccer, captivating enthusiasts with its storied history and serving as a showcase for Europe's premier national teams. As one of the most prestigious international soccer tournaments, it has undergone significant evolution over the years. In its contemporary format, the Euro features 24 top national teams from UEFA member nations, organized into groups and subsequently advancing to knockout stages, culminating in the coronation of the European champion. The Euro is lauded for its riveting contests, strategic brilliance, and the emergence of fresh soccer heroes, providing a grand stage where national pride and fervor reach their zenith, creating indelible moments.

While the Euro is inherently a European affair, its magnetic pull extends across the globe, captivating soccer enthusiasts worldwide. Its high-caliber play and the presence of world-class talent render it a highlight on the international soccer calendar. Over the years, the championship has witnessed an array of victors, ranging from soccer titans to unforeseen underdogs, each contributing to the diverse tapestry of European soccer. More than merely a sporting competition, the Euro holds a distinctive place within European culture, symbolizing a unifying celebration that brings nations and communities together, fostering unity and instilling a sense of pride. On the international soccer stage, the Euro's impact is profound. It provides teams with the opportunity to vie against the very best, with triumph in the tournament serving as a source of immense national pride and glory, thereby playing an influential role in shaping the global soccer landscape.

**FIFA World Cup**

The FIFA World Cup stands as the pinnacle of international soccer, having firmly entrenched itself as a historic and cherished spectacle since its  inauguration in 1930. Recognized as the most prestigious and universally watched sporting event, the World Cup assembles elite national teams from every corner of the globe.

More than merely a soccer competition, the World Cup serves as a worldwide celebration of the sport. Held every four years, it forges connections among nations, cultures, and individuals from diverse backgrounds, all bound together by their shared ardor for soccer. This period marks a global hiatus, as a wave of soccer fervor sweeps through nations, captivating the hearts and minds of people across the planet.

The competition within the World Cup is nothing short of ferocious. Teams engage in a month-long struggle that bears testament to their national pride, with players showcasing their extraordinary talents on the grandest stage of them all. The tournament's format encompasses group stages, knockout rounds, and culminates in the ultimate showdown, where each match possesses the potential to etch its place in history.

The World Cup has served as the stage for the ascent of legendary players who have indelibly shaped the sport. Icons such as Pelé and Diego Maradona have graced this tournament, unveiling their extraordinary soccering prowess to the world.

Beyond the boundaries of sports, the World Cup wields a profound cultural impact. It fosters unity and camaraderie, often uniting rival nations in a shared celebration. Additionally, the event provides host countries with a unique platform to exhibit their culture, traditions, and hospitality to a global audience.

The World Cup transcends its status as a mere sporting event; it stands as a global phenomenon. Attracting billions of viewers, sparking impassioned discussions, and crafting enduring memories, the tournament possesses a distinctive power to inspire and unite people like no other event in the world.

## MESSI'S LIFE

**Early Years**

The story of Lionel Andrés Messi Cuccitini, born on June 24, 1987, in Rosario, Argentina, is a tale of a soccer prodigy who overcame challenges to become a legend. Messi's journey began in a soccer-loving family, where his passion for the game was nurtured from a young age. His father, Jorge Messi, a local steel factory manager, played a crucial role in his early development, coaching Lionel and his brothers at the local club, Grandoli.

From a young age, around four, Messi's talent was evident. He joined Grandoli, where under his father's guidance, he honed his skills. His exceptional abilities soon became apparent, and at the age of 8, he joined Newell's Old Boys, a prominent club in Rosario, where he distinguished himself as a prodigious talent.

However, Messi's journey was not without obstacles. At around 10, he was diagnosed with idiopathic short stature, a growth hormone deficiency, which hindered his physical development. Despite this setback, Messi's family, particularly his mother Celia Cuccitini, provided unwavering emotional support. They approached River Plate, a major Argentinian soccer club, for assistance with his expensive growth hormone treatments.

Unfortunately, River Plate couldn't fund his treatment either.

A pivotal moment came in 2000 when Messi, at 13, moved to Barcelona, Spain, with his family. FC Barcelona had offered to pay for his medical treatments and included him in their youth academy, La Masia. This move marked a new chapter in Messi's life, offering him the platform to showcase his talent on a larger stage. His initial contract with Barcelona, famously signed on a paper napkin, symbolized the club's immediate and decisive commitment to his extraordinary talent.

Lionel Messi's family played an integral role in his journey. He is the third of four children, with a significant age gap between him and his siblings. His older brother Rodrigo, born in 1979, manages Lionel's professional schedule. Matías, five years older, born in 1982, oversees Lionel's charitable foundation. His younger sister, María Sol, born in 1993, maintains a private life but shares a close bond with Lionel.

## The Emergence at FC Barcelona

Lionel Messi's ascent in the world of professional soccer began in February 2002. At the tender age of 13, after joining Barcelona's prestigious youth academy, La Masia, a significant milestone was achieved when he was officially enrolled in the Royal Spanish Football Federation (RFEF). This crucial step not only legitimized his status as a player within the Spanish soccer system but also paved the way for a career that would later redefine the sport.

By June 2004, Messi's potential had crystalized into undeniable talent. Recognizing this, FC Barcelona signed him to his first official contract, solidifying his status as a professional player with the club. This moment marked the beginning of an era, one where Messi would soon become a household name in soccer.

Messi's first appearance for FC Barcelona's first team came on October 16, 2004, in a La Liga match against Espanyol. At just 17, stepping onto the field in the 82nd minute, he marked the beginning of what would be a historic debut in professional soccer. The following year, on May 1, 2005, Messi scored his first official goal for FC Barcelona in a match against Albacete Balompié. Coming off the bench, his skillful lob over the goalkeeper, assisted by Ronaldinho, was a clear indication of the extraordinary talent he possessed.

The 2004/05 season was a harbinger of success for Messi, as he won his first La Liga trophy with FC Barcelona. Although he made only 7 appearances, all as a substitute, and scored a single goal, his impact on the team was already becoming evident.

On November 2, 2005, Messi scored his first UEFA Champions League goal against Panathinaikos. His talent was further showcased in a match against Real Madrid in March 2007, where, at just 19, he became the youngest player to score a hat-trick in the tournament. The 2005-2006 season saw Messi win his first Champions League trophy with FC Barcelona, contributing one goal and one assist in six appearances, although missing the final against Arsenal due to injury.

A defining moment in Messi's early career occurred on March 10, 2007, in an El Clásico match against Real Madrid. At just 19 years old, Messi scored his first career hat-trick, resulting in a 3-3 draw. This performance etched his name in the history books, as he became the first player since Iván Zamorano to score a hat-trick in an El Clásico match. This feat not only underscored his emerging prowess but also highlighted his potential to become one of the greatest players in soccer history.

April 18, 2007, remains etched in soccer history, thanks to Messi's stunning goal in a Copa del Rey semi-final match against Getafe. Starting near the halfway line, he embarked on a breathtaking 60-meter sprint, weaving past five defenders before finishing with an angled shot. This goal is not just remembered as one of the best in soccer history but also revered by Barcelona fans as the finest in their club's storied history.

The 2008-2009 season was also a testament to Messi's growing influence and skill. He was instrumental in FC Barcelona's first-ever treble, securing La Liga, Copa del Rey, and the UEFA Champions League titles. His role as the top scorer in the Champions League during this period solidified his standing as one of the premier soccerers on the global stage.

The 2011-2012 season was a showcase of Messi's goal-scoring prowess. He netted an astonishing 73 goals across all competitions for Barcelona, surpassing Gerd Muller's longstanding record for the most goals in a calendar year and earning his fourth consecutive Ballon d'Or.

March 7, 2012, saw Messi achieve an unprecedented feat in the UEFA Champions League. In a match against Bayer Leverkusen, he scored five goals – a record in the competition. This performance not only highlighted his exceptional skills but also set a new benchmark in Champions League history.

On March 20, 2012, Messi reached another career milestone, becoming Barcelona's all-time top scorer. At only 24, he broke Cesar Rodriguez's 57-year-old record by scoring a hat-trick against Granada, bringing his total to 234 goals for the club.

From 2013 to 2021, Lionel Messi continued to be a central figure in FC Barcelona, contributing significantly to the team's performances. During this period, he displayed consistency in goal-scoring and playmaking, maintaining his status as one of the top players globally. He played a key role in Barcelona's successes, including domestic league titles and notable achievements in European competitions. His influence on the team was characterized by a combination of individual brilliance and teamwork. However, the later years also witnessed some transitions and challenges within the club.

Messi's departure from Barcelona in 2021 marked the end of an era for the club and player, concluding a long and impactful association.

### Paris Saint-Germain & Inter Miami

August 2021 marked the beginning of a new era for Messi as he completed a highly anticipated transfer to Paris Saint-Germain after a 21-year stint with Barcelona. Wearing the number 30 jersey, he formed a formidable attacking trio with Neymar and Kylian Mbappé, helping PSG secure the Ligue 1 title in his debut season. His performance with PSG showcased his continued soccer prowess, contributing both goals and assists, while his adaptability and skill set complemented the team's attacking style of play. His partnership with other star players in the squad became a focal point, significantly influencing the team's dynamics on the field.

Following his time at Paris Saint-Germain, Messi embarked on a new chapter with Major League Soccer club Inter Miami. This significant move in his illustrious career saw him signing a two-and-a-half-season contract, with the possibility of extending it further, potentially keeping him at the club until the 2026 season.

### Performance Alongside Argentina

Throughout his soccer career, Lionel Messi has been a consistent and influential figure for the Argentine national team. From his early days, he demonstrated his talent and versatility on the international stage. Despite facing occasional criticism for not replicating his club success with Barcelona on the national team, he remained a key player, contributing to Argentina's campaigns in various tournaments. His commitment to representing his country has been a notable aspect of his soccer journey.

Messi's international prowess was on full display on August 23, 2008, at the Beijing Olympic Games. In the final against Nigeria, held in the iconic Bird's Nest stadium, he provided a crucial assist, leading Argentina to a 1-0 victory and their second consecutive Olympic soccer gold medal. This win marked the first time since Uruguay in 1924 and 1928 that a team had achieved back-to-back Olympic golds in soccer.

In the 2014 FIFA World Cup held in Brazil, Messi took center stage for Argentina's national team. He led his country to the World Cup final, contributing four goals and numerous assists. Though Argentina finished as runners-up, Messi's extraordinary performances earned him the Golden Ball award, further cementing his legacy as one of the greatest players in the sport's history.

In the 2015 Copa América, Messi led Argentina to the final, showcasing his exceptional skill and leadership. However, the tournament ended in heartbreak as Argentina lost to Chile in a penalty shootout. Despite the defeat, Messi's outstanding performances throughout the tournament earned him the Player of the Tournament award.

In July 2021, Messi realized a lifelong dream by leading Argentina to victory in the Copa América. Defeating Brazil 1-0 in the final, Argentina claimed their first Copa América title in 28 years, and Messi won his first major international trophy. His instrumental role throughout the tournament led to him being named Player of the Tournament and sharing the Golden Boot.

In the 2022 FIFA World Cup final at Lusail Stadium, Messi's legendary status was further cemented. Making a record 26th World Cup finals appearance, he played a pivotal role in the thrilling final. Scoring Argentina's opening goal and again in extra-time, he led his team through a dramatic match against France. The game, tied 3-3 after extra time, was decided in a penalty shootout, with Argentina triumphing 4-2, thus ending a 36-year wait for the World Cup trophy. Messi's extraordinary performances, including 7 goals and 3 assists, earned him the Golden Ball as the tournament's best player.

**International Recognition & Awards**

Messi's talent garnered international recognition in 2005. At the FIFA World Youth Championship, he clinched both the Golden Ball, as the tournament's best  player, and the Golden Shoe, as the top scorer with six goals. However, his journey with the Argentine national team had a rocky start. In a friendly against Hungary in 2005, Messi was sent off just one minute after entering the field, sparking debates about the red card's fairness. Despite this setback, he scored his first international goal in a friendly against Croatia on March 1, 2006.

In 2009, at just 22 years old, Messi won his first Ballon d'Or, an award recognizing the world's best player, following his pivotal role in Barcelona's treble-winning season. His dominance in soccer continued in the following years, retaining the Ballon d'Or in 2010 and then again in 2011, 2012, and 2015. Messi's dominance in the sport was further cemented in December 2019 when he won his sixth Ballon d'Or, setting a new record in the award's history. This honor was a testament to his consistent high-level performances, including scoring 50 goals and providing 18 assists in just 59 games. Messi continued to make history with his seventh and eighth Ballon d'Or wins in 2021 and 2023, respectively, further solidifying his status as one of soccer's all-time greats.

Messi's exceptional talent was again recognized on November 29, 2021, when he won his seventh Ballon d'Or. The following year, in the 2022 Finalissima at Wembley Stadium, Messi demonstrated his brilliance on the international stage. Argentina's victory over Italy, with Messi contributing two assists, underscored his enduring influence and skill in high-stakes matches.

Messi's dominance in soccer extends to the global stage, as evidenced by his two FIFA World Cup Golden Ball awards. These awards, won in 2014 and 2018, are a testament to his exceptional skill and impact at the World Cup, the pinnacle of international soccer. In both tournaments, Messi's performances were pivotal in driving Argentina's campaigns, with his ability to influence games being particularly noteworthy. These accolades not only recognize his individual brilliance but also his capacity to elevate his national team's performance on the world's biggest soccer stage.

Messi's global influence is highlighted by his five FIFA World Player of the Year titles, won in 2009, 2010, 2011, 2012, and 2015. This recognition places him among the most celebrated soccerers in history, emphasizing his impact on the sport at an international level.

In his home country of Argentina, Messi's exceptional talent has been recognized with him being named the Argentine Soccerer of the Year 13 times. This honor underscores his lasting impact on soccer in Argentina and his status as a national icon.

**Noteworthy Records**

**La Liga's All-Time Top Scorer:** On November 22, 2014, Messi made soccer history by becoming the all-time top scorer in La Liga. In a mesmerizing performance against Sevilla, he scored a hat-trick, surpassing Telmo Zarra's 59-year-old record with 252 goals. This achievement not only highlighted his scoring prowess but also firmly entrenched him in the annals of soccer history.

**The Fastest Hat-trick:** Messi's record of 57 career hat-tricks is a demonstration of his consistent excellence. He holds the record for the fastest hat trick in La Liga history, achieving this feat in just 12 minutes during a match against Rayo Vallecano on March 8, 2015.

**A Milestone in El Clásico:** A significant moment in Messi's career occurred on April 23, 2017, when he scored his 500th goal for Barcelona in all competitions. This milestone was achieved in dramatic fashion during an El Clásico match against Real Madrid, where his overtime goal sealed a crucial 3-2 victory.

**Surpassing Pelé's Record:** On December 22, 2020, Messi achieved another historic milestone by becoming the top goalscorer with a single club, surpassing Pelé's record of 643 goals with Santos. Messi's 644th goal, scored in a victory over Real Valladolid, broke a record that had stood for 46 years.

**Record-Breaking Ballon d'Or Wins:** Lionel Messi's illustrious career is marked by multiple Ballon d'Or victories, a prestigious individual accolade awarded annually by France Football. His first triumph came in 2009, followed by consecutive wins in 2010 and 2011. Messi continued his dominance, claiming the award in 2012 and 2015. After a brief hiatus, he secured the Ballon d'Or once again in 2019, setting a new record with six wins. Messi added to this remarkable feat with his seventh Ballon d'Or in 2021 and an eighth in 2023, reaffirming his status as one of the greatest soccerers in history. Each victory reflects his consistent excellence and enduring impact on the global soccer stage.

**Holder of 41 Guinness World Records:** Messi's name is associated with an impressive 41 Guinness World Records, a testament to his extraordinary achievements in soccer. Notable records include winning the most Man of the Match awards at the FIFA World Cup (11), being the first person to assist in five different FIFA World Cups, making the most FIFA World Cup appearances as a captain (19), and having the most appearances in FIFA World Cup tournaments by a male player, participating in 5 different editions. These records not only highlight his consistency and excellence on the global stage but also his leadership and influence in the sport.

**Playing Style**

Over the years, Messi's playing style has undergone a remarkable transformation. Initially celebrated as a nimble and skillful winger at FC Barcelona, he seamlessly combined extraordinary dribbling skills with precise finishing. Gradually, he evolved into a more central attacking role, often operating as a 'false nine,' merging his playmaking abilities with prolific goal-scoring. During his tenure at Paris Saint-Germain, Messi continued to adapt, embracing a more creative midfield role while maintaining his scoring threat. His expressed desire to continue playing at the highest level into his late 30s underscores his dedication to maintaining top physical fitness and performance standards throughout his career.

Messi's signature move, earning him the nickname "La Pulga" (The Flea), showcases his exceptional agility and quickness. Characterized by rapid changes in direction while maintaining close control of the ball, this move has become a hallmark of his playing style. His low center of gravity, coupled with extraordinary balance and dribbling skills, enables him to weave through tight spaces and evade multiple defenders, often leaving them bewildered in his wake.

### Remarkable Skills

Lionel Messi's career has been marked by a series of impressive achievements and skills that highlight his impact on soccer.

**Free-Kick Expertise:** Messi's prowess in free-kicks is evident in his 65 successful conversions. This skill has been a fundamental aspect of his play, contributing significantly to his team's success.

**Consistent Scorer:** Remarkably, Messi has scored goals in every minute of a soccer match, demonstrating his consistent threat in front of the goal throughout the entire duration of a game.

**Physical Attributes and Scoring Versatility:** Despite his height of 5 feet 7 inches (1.7 meters), Messi's performance has been on par with, or surpassed, taller players, challenging the notion that physical stature is a key determinant of success in soccer. His ability to score with various parts of his body is notable, with 23 headed goals and 75 right-footed goals, adding to his dominant left-footed scoring ability.

**Penalty Conversion:** Messi's effectiveness is also seen in penalty situations, where he converted 77 penalties for Barcelona, showcasing his skill in high-pressure scenarios.

**Goal Distribution:** His scoring distribution is balanced, with 215 goals from the left field, 215 from the right, and 104 from the center. Notably, 385 of his goals have come from within the 6-yard box, reflecting his proficiency in close-range scoring. Additionally, he has demonstrated his ability to score from long-range, with 24 goals from beyond the 18-yard box.

**Providing for Teammates:** Beyond scoring, Messi has recorded 205 assists during his time at Barcelona, for example, indicating his ability to contribute to his team's offensive play beyond just scoring goals.

Messi's exceptional agility and speed on the field are products of a structured and disciplined workout plan. His training regimen is designed to optimize both linear and multidirectional speed, incorporating exercises like lunges, hamstring stretches, pillar skips, skipping ropes, and squats. Agility is a key focus, with diagonal hurdles and cone drills forming integral parts of his routine. Each session concludes with proper hydration and a cooldown jog, emphasizing the importance of recovery in his physical preparation.

His lifestyle choices, particularly his diet, play a fundamental role in his performance. Messi follows a diet focused on hydration and whole foods, avoiding sugar and fried foods. His typical meal includes roasted chicken with root vegetables, with a limited intake of meat during training periods. He emphasizes the importance of protein shakes and water for digestion, underscoring his commitment to maintaining top physical fitness.

## Rituals & Preferences

Messi is known to have a few superstitions that are part of his pre-game rituals. One such superstition is entering the field with his right foot first. He also wears the same shin guards that his grandmother bought him as a child, a touching homage to her influence in his early life. Before stepping onto the pitch, Messi typically kisses his tattoo of his mother's lips, further paying tribute to her and carrying her presence with him in every game.

Messi's iconic goal celebration, pointing towards the sky, is a deeply personal tribute to his late grandmother, Celia. She was instrumental in nurturing his passion for soccer during his early years. Her encouragement played a significant role in his development as a young soccerer. Despite her passing in 1998, Messi's celebration ensures that her memory and influence continue to be a part of his journey, reflecting the deep bond they shared.

In a candid interview with Paris Saint-Germain, Messi revealed his preference for the role of a second striker. He articulated a fondness for playing centrally, just behind the lead striker, a position where he feels most at home. Messi's inclination for this role stems from his desire to be continuously involved in the game, underlining his passion for contributing actively to his team's play. His statement, "I like to always be in contact with the ball," reflects his playmaking ethos and his enjoyment in orchestrating the game, making crucial passes, and setting up goals.

**Personal Life & Interests**

Lionel Messi's illustrious career is a blend of remarkable professional achievements and personal elements that offer deeper insights into his character and preferences, contributing to his multifaceted persona.

His personal life, particularly his relationship with Antonela Roccuzzo, is a demonstration of his grounded and loving nature. Both hailing from Rosario, Argentina, they met in childhood and began dating in their teens. Their relationship culminated in a grand wedding in 2017, attended by numerous celebrities and soccer stars. The couple has three sons, Thiago, Mateo, and Ciro, who have shown an early interest in soccer, much to the anticipation of fans worldwide.

During his iconic tenure with FC Barcelona, the city became a second home for Messi and his family. They immersed themselves in the local culture and community, embracing everything the Catalan capital had to offer beyond the soccer pitch.

Exploring another facet of Lionel Messi's diverse interests, his passion for art is evident in his collection, which includes works by Catalan surrealist Joan Miró, known for their abstract and playful nature. This collection offers insight into Messi's appreciation for art that challenges reality.

Concerning Messi's tattoos, they are more than just body art; they are deeply personal. On his left shoulder, he has a tattoo of his mother's face, symbolizing her unwavering support throughout his life and career. Additionally, he has tattooed the name of his firstborn son, Thiago, on his calf, reflecting the strong bond and immense love he holds for his son.

Lionel is also known for being a pet lover. He often shares his affection for dogs on social media, particularly his Dogue de Bordeaux, a breed known for its loyalty and affectionate nature. His social media posts frequently feature pictures and videos of his beloved pet. Beyond his love for pets, Messi has a musical side too. He plays the guitar during his leisure time, using music as a form of relaxation and a way to unwind from the demands of his high-profile career.

Native to Rosario, Argentina, Lionel Messi primarily communicates in Spanish. Throughout his extensive tenure at FC Barcelona, Messi became familiar with Catalan, the predominant language in the region. Despite this, he has not yet acquired proficiency in additional languages like English, often opting to express himself in Spanish during public appearances and interviews. This choice reflects his comfort with his native language and cultural roots, despite his global presence.

In navigating the often extroverted landscape of professional sports, Lionel Messi's renowned introverted personality sets him apart. Known for his inherent shyness and reserved demeanor, particularly evident in the early stages of his career, Messi's distinctive approach to fame is reflected in his modest goal celebrations and a preference for a private life, shielded from the constant media spotlight. This unique aspect of his personality, in contrast to the more common public personas of professional athletes, has endeared him to fans who value his commitment to soccer and personal integrity over the allure of celebrity status.

**Philanthropy**

In the latter stages of Lionel Messi's career, a period seamlessly intertwined with his personal life and off-field contributions, monumental achievements unfold alongside a deep commitment to family and philanthropy. Messi's impact transcends the boundaries of soccer, extending far beyond the pitch. The genesis of this broader influence lies in the Leo Messi Foundation, a testament to his dedication to improving the lives of disadvantaged children, especially in healthcare and education. Through his foundation, Messi has spearheaded various initiatives, including the construction of schools and medical facilities. Furthermore, his active engagement in charitable activities beyond the foundation encompasses contributions to disaster relief and healthcare projects. These humanitarian efforts have garnered numerous accolades, underscoring Messi's role as a positive influence both on and off the field.

## Off the Field Ventures

Lionel Messi's career, marked by staggering achievements on the field, is complemented by his ventures into fashion, hospitality, and art, as well as his record-breaking performances. Beyond his soccer prowess and endorsements, Messi expanded his influence into the fashion industry with "The Messi Store." This venture reflects his personal style and taste, offering a range of clothing and apparel that resonates with his fans and fashion enthusiasts.

Messi's passion for design is further showcased through "The Messi Collection," a collaboration with architect Luis Galliussi. This unique furniture line blends aesthetics, functionality, and comfort, allowing fans to incorporate Messi's distinctive style into their homes.

Messi's entrepreneurial spirit also extends to the culinary world with the "Bellavista del Jardín del Norte" restaurant chain in Argentina. These establishments are celebrated for their delightful ambiance and a menu rich in Argentine culinary traditions, attracting both locals and international visitors and contributing to Messi's portfolio outside of soccer.

In Barcelona, Messi's partnership with the Majestic Hotel Group led to the creation of the "Majestic Messi" hotel. Located in the heart of Barcelona, this luxury hotel caters to tourists seeking cultural experiences and premium service, thus significantly contributing to the local tourism and economy.

On a broader international scale, Messi is renowned for his partnerships with major brands such as Adidas, Pepsi, and Huawei. These endorsements not only contribute significantly to his income but also establish him as a prominent global icon in the sports industry.

**Fun, Random Facts**

• Messi's admiration for former Argentine playmaker Pablo Aimar is a notable aspect of his soccer journey. Growing up, Messi looked up to Aimar, and their paths crossed in La Liga, leading to a memorable encounter where Aimar gifted his shirt to a 17-year-old Messi. This gesture left an indelible mark on Messi and symbolized his admiration for Aimar. Interestingly, Aimar later became an assistant coach for the Argentina national team, contributing to their success in the 2022 World Cup, adding a unique dimension to their relationship.

• During his time at Barcelona's La Masia academy, Messi caught the attention of Arsenal's former manager Arsene Wenger. Wenger's interest in signing Messi highlights the early recognition of his talent, but Messi's commitment to Barcelona saw him decline the offer and continue his growth with the Catalan club.

• In a unique tribute to his soccer prowess, Messi's left foot was immortalized in a 25-carat gold cast. This symbol of his impact on the sport was valued at $5.3 million and sold to support those affected by the 2011 tsunami in Japan, demonstrating how his legacy extends beyond the pitch.

• Despite his numerous awards, Messi has never won the Golden Foot Award, an accolade recognizing players' achievements and personality.

• In his career, Messi has received three red cards, two with Argentina and one with FC Barcelona, rare incidents in an otherwise disciplined career.

• An interesting aspect of Messi's personal life is his family connection to former Barcelona teammate Bojan Krkic. They are fourth cousins, with shared ancestors dating back to the 19th century in Catalonia. This connection adds a familial dimension to their professional relationship and their shared soccer journey.

• Away from the limelight of professional soccer, Messi displays endearing traits that make him relatable to fans. Former Argentina teammate Pablo Zabaleta shared light-hearted anecdotes, revealing that Messi is less adept at playing FIFA video games, often choosing Chelsea as his preferred team. Zabaleta also humorously commented on Messi's modest culinary skills and dancing abilities, portraying a side of Messi that is more personal and distinct from his soccer identity.

• In a high-profile legal case, Messi faced a 21-month prison sentence for tax fraud, which was later converted into a fine by Spanish courts. He was required to pay €252,000, which equates to €400 for each day of the original sentence. This case arose from accusations of defrauding Spain of €4.1 million between 2007 and 2009 through the use of tax havens to conceal earnings from image rights. Similarly, his father, Jorge Messi, also faced legal repercussions, with his 15-month sentence being replaced by a €180,000 fine.

• Messi's digital representation in the FIFA video game series mirrors his real-life success. From FIFA 06 to FIFA 23, his ratings have consistently been among the highest, reflecting his status as one of the top players in the world. Notably, Messi has appeared on the cover of soccer video games a record 12 times.

• Messi is synonymous with the number 10 jersey, a symbol of playmaking excellence and leadership in soccer. He inherited this number from Ronaldinho at FC Barcelona in 2008, a gesture that symbolized the passing of the baton to Messi as the team's leading playmaker and a key figure in soccer. At Paris Saint-Germain, Messi initially chose number 30, reminiscent of his first professional number at Barcelona, before returning to the iconic number 10. This jersey number has become a significant part of Messi's identity, representing his status as one of the greatest players in the history of the sport.

## Digital Presence

Lionel Messi's life extends far beyond the soccer pitch, embodying a richness and diversity reflective of his multifaceted career. His journey is characterized by distinct symbols, unique habits, a robust digital presence, and a lifestyle that significantly contributes to his on-field success.

Surpassing a remarkable milestone, Messi has garnered over 100 million followers on Instagram, underscoring his global popularity and influence. Within the digital realm, his account seamlessly weaves together personal moments with his family, highlights from his illustrious soccer career, and diverse endorsements, providing fans with a captivating glimpse into both his professional and personal spheres.

# 3

## TRIVIA QUESTIONS

Embark on a journey through the remarkable life of Lionel Messi with this trivia. Each question is a gateway to uncovering the incredible milestones, and anecdotes that define the legacy of one of soccer's greatest maestros. Test your knowledge and discover the secrets behind Messi's extraordinary career.

1. What is Lionel Messi's full birth name?

a) Lionel Andrés Di María

b) Lionel Messi

c) Lionel Andrés Messi

d) Lionel Andrés Messi Cuccitini


2. What was Lionel Messi's father's occupation?

a) Soccer Coach

b) Steel Factory Manager

c) Professional Soccerer

d) School Teacher


3. What role did Lionel Messi's mother play in his development?

a) She was his first soccer coach

b) She managed his early career

c) She provided strong emotional support

d) She was a professional athlete


4. How many siblings does Lionel Messi have?

a) One

b) Two

c) Three

d) Four

5. At what age did Lionel Messi start playing soccer?

a) 3 years old

b) 4 years old

c) 5 years old

d) 6 years old

6. Which club did Lionel Messi join at age 8?

a) FC Barcelona

b) River Plate

c) Boca Juniors

d) Newell's Old Boys

7. What medical condition was Lionel Messi diagnosed with at the age of 10?

a) Idiopathic short stature

b) Asthma

c) Osteoporosis

d) Anemia

8. Which soccer club did Messi's family approach for help with his medical treatments?

a) Boca Juniors

b) River Plate

c) Atlético Madrid

d) Independiente

9. At what age did Lionel Messi move to Barcelona, Spain?

a) 10

b) 11

c) 12

d) 13

10. How was Messi's initial contract with FC Barcelona signed?

a) On a formal contract paper

b) In a legal office

c) On a paper napkin

d) Digitally

11. At what age was Lionel Messi officially enrolled in the Royal Spanish Football Federation (RFEF)?

a) 11

b) 12

c) 13

d) 14


12. When did Messi sign his first official contract with FC Barcelona?

a) May 2003

b) June 2004

c) July 2005

d) August 2006


13. When did Lionel Messi make his official debut for FC Barcelona's first team?

a) October 2003

b) November 2004

c) October 2004

d) September 2005


14. When did Messi score his first official goal for FC Barcelona?

a) April 2005

b) May 2005

c) June 2005

d) July 2005


15. In which season did Messi win his first La Liga trophy with FC Barcelona?

a) 2003/04

b) 2004/05

c) 2005/06

d) 2006/07


16. Which awards did Messi win at the FIFA World Youth Championship in 2005?

a) Golden Boot and Silver Ball

b) Golden Shoe and Silver Ball

c) Golden Ball and Golden Shoe

d) Silver Ball and Silver Shoe


17. Against which team did Messi make his debut for the Argentine national team?

a) Brazil

b) Hungary

c) Croatia

d) Portugal


18. When did Messi score his first UEFA Champions League goal?

a) October 2005

b) November 2005

c) December 2005

d) January 2006

19. In which season did Messi win his first Champions League trophy with FC Barcelona?

a) 2004-2005

b) 2005-2006

c) 2006-2007

d) 2007-2008

20. In which match did Messi score his first career hat-trick?

a) Against Espanyol

b) Against Arsenal

c) Against Real Madrid

d) Against Chelsea

21. On which date did Lionel Messi score a goal often regarded as one of the best in soccer history in a Copa del Rey match against Getafe?

a) April 16, 2007

b) April 18, 2007

c) April 20, 2007

d) April 22, 2007

22. In which season did Messi help FC Barcelona achieve their first-ever treble?

a) 2006-2007

b) 2007-2008

c) 2008-2009

d) 2009-2010

23. When did Messi play a crucial role in Argentina's Olympic gold medal victory at the Beijing Games?

a) 2006

b) 2008

c) 2010

d) 2012

24. At what age did Lionel Messi win his first Ballon d'Or?

a) 20

b) 21

c) 22

d) 23

25. In which year did Messi win his second consecutive Ballon d'Or?

a) 2008

b) 2009

c) 2010

d) 2011

26. How many consecutive years did Messi win the Ballon d'Or from 2009?

a) Two

b) Three

c) Four

d) Five

27. When did Messi score five goals in a single UEFA Champions League match?

a) March 5, 2012

b) March 7, 2012

c) March 9, 2012

d) March 11, 2012

28. How many goals did Messi score in the 2011-2012 season, breaking Gerd Muller's record?

a) 68

b) 70

c) 73

d) 75

29. At what age did Messi become Barcelona's all-time top scorer?

a) 22

b) 23

c) 24

d) 25

30. In which FIFA World Cup did Messi lead Argentina to the final and win the Golden Ball award?

a) 2010

b) 2014

c) 2018

d) 2022

31. When did Lionel Messi become the all-time top scorer in La Liga?

a) November 2013

b) November 2014

c) November 2015

d) November 2016

32. What was the outcome of the 2015 Copa América final for Argentina?

a) Victory in regular time

b) Victory on penalties

c) Defeat in regular time

d) Defeat on penalties

33. When did Messi score his 500th goal for Barcelona?

a) April 2017

b) May 2017

c) June 2017

d) July 2017

34. How many times has Messi won the Ballon d'Or as of December 2019?

a) Four

b) Five

c) Six

d) Seven

35. When did Messi surpass Pelé's record to become the top goalscorer with a single club?

a) December 2019

b) December 2020

c) January 2021

d) February 2021

36. What achievement did Messi accomplish in the Copa América in July 2021?

a) Winning the Golden Boot

b) Winning his first major international trophy

c) Scoring the winning goal in the final

d) All of the above

37. In what year did Messi transfer to Paris Saint-Germain (PSG)?

a) 2020

b) 2021

c) 2022

d) 2023

38. Which squad number did Messi initially choose at PSG?

a) 10

b) 19

c) 30

d) 33

39. How many Ballon d'Or awards had Messi won by November 2021?

a) Six

b) Seven

c) Eight

d) Nine

40. In which event did Messi play a pivotal role for Argentina against Italy in 2022?

a) UEFA Champions League

b) Copa América

c) Finalissima

d) World Cup

41. How many World Cup finals appearances had Messi made by the 2022 FIFA World Cup?

a) 24

b) 25

c) 26

d) 27

42. In which league did Messi sign after leaving Paris Saint-Germain (PSG)?

a) English Premier League

b) La Liga

c) Major League Soccer (MLS)

d) Serie A

43. How did Lionel Messi and Antonela Roccuzzo first meet?

a) At a soccer match

b) Through mutual friends

c) As children in Rosario

d) In Barcelona


44. In which year did Lionel Messi marry Antonela Roccuzzo?

a) 2015

b) 2016

c) 2017

d) 2018


45. How many sons do Lionel Messi and Antonela Roccuzzo have?

a) One

b) Two

c) Three

d) Four


46. Which city served as a second home for Lionel Messi during his time at FC Barcelona?

a) Madrid

b) Rosario

c) Barcelona

d) Paris

47. What is the primary focus of the Leo Messi Foundation?

a) Sports training for youth

b) Healthcare initiatives for children

c) Disaster relief efforts

d) Providing soccer equipment

48. In addition to his foundation, what other charitable activities has Messi been involved in?

a) Environmental conservation

b) Animal rights activism

c) Disaster relief and healthcare

d) Political campaigns

49. What type of brands has Messi endorsed?

a) Automotive and luxury goods

b) Sportswear and technology

c) Fast food and beverages

d) Financial services and banking

50. What was Messi's role in Argentina's victory in the 2022 FIFA World Cup final?

a) Scoring a hat-trick

b) Assisting the winning goal

c) Scoring in the penalty shootout

d) Goalkeeping in the shootout

51. What type of brand did Lionel Messi launch in the fashion industry?

a) A luxury watch brand

b) A sports apparel brand

c) A clothing and apparel brand

d) A footwear brand

52. What is the name of the restaurant chain owned by Lionel Messi and his family in Argentina?

a) Messi's Delicacies

b) Argentine Flavors by Messi

c) Bellavista del Jardín del Norte

d) El Rincón de Messi

53. What unique aspect is associated with the "Majestic Messi" hotel in Barcelona?

a) Soccer-themed decorations

b) A museum dedicated to Messi

c) Emphasis on exclusivity and elegance

d) A sports complex with soccer fields

54. Which artist's works are prominently featured in Lionel Messi's art collection?

a) Pablo Picasso

b) Salvador Dalí

c) Joan Miró

d) Frida Kahlo

55. In La Liga, at what age did Lionel Messi receive a shirt as a gift from Pablo Aimar?

a) 15

b) 17

c) 20

d) 22

56. What type of artwork does Lionel Messi's collection predominantly feature?

a) Classical portraits

b) Abstract and playful pieces

c) Renaissance sculptures

d) Modernist installations

57. What is "The Messi Collection" known for?

a) A series of sports memorabilia

b) A unique line of watches

c) A distinctive furniture line

d) A collection of soccer kits

58. How many hat-tricks has Lionel Messi scored throughout his career?

a) 47

b) 57

c) 67

d) 77

59. What is Messi's record for the fastest hat-trick in La Liga?

a) 10 minutes

b) 12 minutes

c) 15 minutes

d) 20 minutes

60. How many free-kick goals has Messi scored?

a) 55

b) 60

c) 65

d) 70

61. In which minutes of a soccer match has Lionel Messi scored goals?

a) Only in the first half

b) Only in the second half

c) From the 1st to the 45th minute

d) Every minute, from the first to the last

62. How tall is Lionel Messi?

a) 5 feet 5 inches (1.65 meters)

b) 5 feet 7 inches (1.70 meters)

c) 5 feet 9 inches (1.75 meters)

d) 5 feet 11 inches (1.80 meters)

63. How many goals has Messi scored using his head?

a) 13

b) 23

c) 33

d) 43

64. How many goals has Messi scored with his right foot?

a) 55

b) 65

c) 75

d) 85

65. How many penalties has Messi converted for Barcelona?

a) 57

b) 67

c) 77

d) 87

66. From which field positions has Messi scored exactly 215 goals each?

a) Left and right fields

b) Center and right fields

c) Left and center fields

d) Behind the midline and left fields

67. How many of Messi's goals were scored from within the 6-yard box?

a) 285

b) 385

c) 485

d) 585

68. How many goals has Messi scored from beyond the 18-yard box?

a) 14

b) 24

c) 34

d) 44

69. How many assists has Messi recorded during his time at Barcelona?

a) 105

b) 205

c) 305

d) 405

70. In the digital realm, how does Messi's Instagram account offer a glimpse into his life?

a) Strictly professional moments

b) Exclusive family moments

c) Personal and professional moments

d) Highlights of endorsements only

71. How does Messi's approach to fame differ from the common public personas of professional athletes?

a) He seeks constant media attention

b) He maintains a private life

c) He avoids soccer commitments

d) He embraces celebrity status

72. What is Lionel Messi's signature move, earning him the nickname "La Pulga" (The Flea)?

a) A powerful header

b) A long-range shot

c) Exceptional agility and quick changes in direction

d) A sliding tackle

73. According to Messi, what reflects his playmaking ethos and enjoyment on the field?

a) Scoring spectacular goals

b) Making crucial passes and setting up goals

c) Defending aggressively

d) A preference for playing on the wings

74. How many FIFA World Player of the Year titles has Messi won?

a) 3

b) 4

c) 5

d) 6

75. How many times has Messi been named Argentine Soccerer of the Year?

a) 10 times

b) 11 times

c) 12 times

d) 13 times

76. What unique tribute was made to Messi's left foot?

a) A statue in Barcelona

b) A solid 25-carat gold cast

c) A signature shoe line

d) An imprint at Camp Nou

77. Which prestigious soccer award has Messi never won?

a) Ballon d'Or

b) Golden Foot award

c) FIFA World Player of the Year

d) UEFA Best Player in Europe

78. How many red cards has Messi received in his career?

a) One

b) Two

c) Three

d) Four

79. Which club did Arsene Wenger try to sign Messi for?

a) Manchester United

b) Arsenal

c) Chelsea

d) Real Madrid

80. What is the family connection between Messi and Bojan Krkic?

a) Second cousins

b) Third cousins

c) Fourth cousins

d) Not related

81. How many times has Messi been awarded the FIFA World Cup Golden Ball?

a) Once

b) Twice

c) Three times

d) Never

82. What position does Messi prefer to play, as stated in his interview with PSG?

a) Winger

b) Striker

c) Central midfielder

d) Second striker

83. What is one of Messi's lesser-known skills according to his former teammate Pablo Zabaleta?

a) Cooking

b) Dancing

c) Playing FIFA on PlayStation

d) Playing guitar

84. Messi's goal celebration, pointing to the sky, is a tribute to whom?

a) His father

b) His grandmother

c) His mother

d) His son

85. Which former Argentine player did Messi idolize as a young soccer enthusiast?

a) Diego Maradona

b) Gabriel Batistuta

c) Pablo Aimar

d) Juan Román Riquelme

86. What significant tribute does Messi have tattooed on his left shoulder?

a) His father's portrait

b) His mother's face

c) His son's name

d) A soccer

87. One of Messi's superstitions involves how he enters the field. What does he do?

a) Ties his shoelaces twice

b) Enters with his right foot first

c) Touches the grass before playing

d) Wears a specific wristband

88. What milestone did Messi achieve on Instagram?

a) 50 million followers

b) 75 million followers

c) 100 million followers

d) 150 million followers

89. What type of dog does Lionel Messi own?

a) Labrador Retriever

b) Dogue de Bordeaux

c) German Shepherd

d) Golden Retriever

90. Aside from soccer, what musical talent does Messi possess?

a) Singing

b) Playing the guitar

c) Playing the piano

d) Drumming

91. How is Messi's signature move characterized?

a) Slow and deliberate

b) Rapid changes in direction with close ball control

c) Long, powerful strides

d) Aerial acrobatics

92. How many times has Messi appeared on the cover of video game franchises like FIFA and eFootball?

a) 8 times

b) 10 times

c) 12 times

d) 15 times

93. What is the focus of Lionel Messi's diet?

a) Low-carb, high-protein

b) Vegan

c) Hydration and whole foods

d) High-carb, low-fat

94. Messi primarily communicates in which language?

a) English

b) Catalan

c) Spanish

d) French

95. Which exercise is NOT part of Messi's workout plan?

a) Lunges

b) Squats

c) Pilates

d) Skipping ropes

96. What was the outcome of Lionel Messi's prison sentence for tax fraud?

a) It was fully served

b) Converted into community service

c) Converted into a fine

d) Pardoned by the Spanish government

97. Which jersey number did Messi inherit from Ronaldinho at FC Barcelona?

a) 7

b) 10

c) 30

d) 8

98. Which trait is Lionel Messi especially known for?

a) Extroverted personality

b) Introverted personality

c) Aggressive playing style

d) Flamboyant lifestyle

99. How many Guinness World Records does Lionel Messi hold?

a) 25

b) 31

c) 41

d) 50

100. Which of these statements best describes Messi's signature playing style?

a) Power and physical strength

b) Height and heading ability

c) Agility and quickness

d) Long-range shooting prowess


101. In his career, Messi transitioned from playing as a winger to which role?

a) Goalkeeper

b) Central defender

c) Creative midfielder

d) False nine

## 4

# TRIVIA ANSWERS

Discover the essence of Lionel Messi's greatness with the following answers. Unveil the secrets behind his iconic moments and achievements, gaining a glimpse into the extraordinary journey of the soccer legend.

1. d) Lionel Andrés Messi Cuccitini

2. b) Steel Factory Manager

3. c) She provided strong emotional support

4. c) Three

5. b) 4 years old

6. d) Newell's Old Boys

7. a) Idiopathic short stature

8. b) River Plate

9. d) 13

10. c) On a paper napkin

11. c) 13

12. b) June 2004

13. c) October 2004

14. b) May 2005

15. b) 2004/05

16. c) Golden Ball and Golden Shoe

17. b) Hungary

18. b) November 2005

19. b) 2005-2006

20. c) Against Real Madrid

21. b) April 18, 2007

22. c) 2008-2009

23. b) 2008

24. c) 22

25. c) 2010

26. c) Four

27. b) March 7, 2012

28. c) 73

29. c) 24

30. b) 2014


31. b) November 2014

32. d) Defeat on penalties

33. a) April 2017

34. c) Six

35. b) December 2020

36. b) Winning his first major international trophy

37. b) 2021

38. c) 30

39. b) Seven

40. c) Finalissima


41. c) 26

42. c) Major League Soccer (MLS)

43. c) As children in Rosario

44. c) 2017

45. c) Three

46. c) Barcelona

47. b) Healthcare initiatives for children

48. c) Disaster relief and healthcare

49. b) Sportswear and technology

50. c) Scoring in the penalty shootout


51. c) A clothing and apparel brand

52. c) Bellavista del Jardín del Norte

53. c) Emphasis on exclusivity and elegance

54. c) Joan Miró

55. b) 17

56. b) Abstract and playful pieces

57. c) A distinctive furniture line

58. b) 57

59. b) 12 minutes

60. c) 65


61. d) Every minute, from the first to the last

62. b) 5 feet 7 inches (1.70 meters)

63. b) 23

64. c) 75

65. c) 77

66. a) Left and right fields

67. b) 385

68. b) 24

69. b) 205

70. c) Personal and professional moments

71. b) He maintains a private life

72. c) Exceptional agility and quick changes in direction

73. b) Making crucial passes and setting up goals

74. c) 5

75. d) 13 times

76. b) A solid 25-carat gold cast

77. b) Golden Foot award

78. c) Three

79. b) Arsenal

80. c) Fourth cousins

81. b) Twice

82. d) Second striker

83. c) Playing FIFA on PlayStation

84. b) His grandmother

85. c) Pablo Aimar

86. b) His mother's face

87. b) Enters with his right foot first

88. c) 100 million followers

89. b) Dogue de Bordeaux

90 b) Playing the guitar

91. b) Rapid changes in direction with close ball control

92. c) 12 times

93. c) Hydration and whole foods

94. c) Spanish

95. c) Pilates

96. c) Converted into a fine

97. b) 10

98. b) Introverted personality

99. c) 41

100. c) Agility and quickness

101. d) False nine

# MESSI QUIZ SCORECARD

Score ___/101

### 1-20: Beginner Fan

You're just starting to learn about Messi. Keep exploring his story, and your knowledge will surely grow!

## 21-40: Rising Star

You have a budding understanding of Lionel Messi. Continue your journey, and you'll uncover even more about this soccer legend!

## 41-60: In the Game

You're getting to know Messi quite well. Stay curious, and you'll soon be a Messi aficionado!

## 61-80: Messi Enthusiast

Impressive! You have a solid grasp of Lionel Messi's career and life. Keep up the good work, and you'll soon be a top expert!

## 81-100: Messi Expert

Fantastic! Your knowledge about Lionel Messi is remarkable. You're nearly at the pinnacle of Messi expertise!

## 101: Ultimate Messi Fan

Incredible! You've achieved the highest score, proving your status as the ultimate Lionel Messi fan. You truly know him inside and out!

# BONUS: FREE RONALDO BOOK

Are you ready to delve into the next thrilling book in the series, absolutely free? Get ready to explore the captivating world of yet another soccer legend! Just use your smartphone or tablet to scan the QR code below, then follow the simple prompts to receive the PDF.

Made in the USA
Columbia, SC
21 November 2025

73941775R00050